50 Vegan Curry Recipes for Home

By: Kelly Johnson

Table of Contents

- Chickpea Curry
- Lentil Spinach Curry
- Cauliflower Curry
- Sweet Potato Curry
- Thai Green Curry
- Coconut Curry with Tofu
- Mushroom Curry
- Eggplant Curry
- Red Lentil Curry
- Butternut Squash Curry
- Potato Curry
- Vegan Butter Chicken Curry
- Jackfruit Curry
- Black Bean Curry
- Pumpkin Curry
- Pea and Potato Curry
- Okra Curry
- Spinach and Potato Curry
- Masoor Dal Curry
- Chickpea and Spinach Curry
- Tofu Tikka Masala
- Mushroom and Pea Curry
- Cashew Curry
- Zucchini Curry
- Mixed Vegetable Curry
- Kidney Bean Curry
- Vegan Korma
- Spicy Tomato Curry
- Carrot and Lentil Curry
- Tempeh Curry
- Cabbage Curry
- Bell Pepper Curry
- Chickpea and Cauliflower Curry
- Coconut Chickpea Curry
- Peanut Curry
- Beetroot Curry
- Quinoa Curry
- Lentil and Pumpkin Curry
- Turmeric Tofu Curry
- Vegan Rogan Josh

- Green Bean Curry
- Tamarind Curry
- Vegan Paneer Curry (with tofu or paneer substitute)
- Brussels Sprouts Curry
- Avocado Curry
- Mango Curry
- Vegan Bhuna
- Ratatouille Curry
- Lemon and Lentil Curry
- Vegan Jalfrezi

Chickpea Curry

Ingredients:

- 2 cans (15 oz each) chickpeas, drained and rinsed
- 1 onion, diced
- 3 cloves garlic, minced
- 1-inch piece of ginger, grated
- 1 can (14 oz) diced tomatoes
- 1 can (14 oz) coconut milk
- 1 tablespoon curry powder
- 1 teaspoon ground cumin
- 1 teaspoon ground coriander
- 1/2 teaspoon turmeric powder
- 1/4 teaspoon cayenne pepper (optional, for heat)
- Salt, to taste
- Black pepper, to taste
- 2 tablespoons cooking oil
- Fresh cilantro, chopped (for garnish)
- Cooked rice or naan bread (for serving)

Instructions:

1. Heat the cooking oil in a large skillet or pot over medium heat. Add the diced onion and sauté until translucent, about 5 minutes.
2. Add the minced garlic and grated ginger to the skillet. Cook for another 2 minutes until fragrant.
3. Stir in the curry powder, ground cumin, ground coriander, turmeric powder, and cayenne pepper (if using). Cook for 1 minute to toast the spices.
4. Add the diced tomatoes (with their juices) to the skillet. Stir well to combine with the onion and spice mixture.
5. Pour in the coconut milk and stir until everything is well combined.
6. Add the drained and rinsed chickpeas to the skillet. Stir to coat the chickpeas with the curry sauce.
7. Season with salt and black pepper, to taste. Allow the curry to simmer for 15-20 minutes, stirring occasionally, until the sauce has thickened slightly.
8. Taste and adjust seasoning if needed.
9. Once the curry is ready, remove from heat and garnish with fresh chopped cilantro.
10. Serve the chickpea curry hot with cooked rice or naan bread.

Enjoy your homemade Chickpea Curry!

Lentil Spinach Curry

Ingredients:

- 1 cup dried lentils (any variety), rinsed and drained
- 4 cups vegetable broth or water
- 1 tablespoon olive oil or coconut oil
- 1 onion, finely chopped
- 3 cloves garlic, minced
- 1 tablespoon grated ginger
- 1 teaspoon ground cumin
- 1 teaspoon ground coriander
- 1 teaspoon turmeric powder
- 1/2 teaspoon chili powder (adjust to taste)
- 1/2 teaspoon garam masala
- Salt to taste
- 1 can (14 oz) diced tomatoes
- 1 can (14 oz) coconut milk
- 4 cups fresh spinach leaves, washed and chopped
- Fresh cilantro, chopped (for garnish)
- Cooked rice or naan bread (for serving)

Instructions:

1. In a large pot, combine the lentils and vegetable broth or water. Bring to a boil, then reduce the heat and let it simmer for about 20-25 minutes, or until lentils are tender. Drain any excess liquid and set aside.
2. In a separate large skillet or pot, heat the olive oil over medium heat. Add the chopped onion and cook until softened, about 5 minutes.
3. Add the minced garlic and grated ginger to the skillet. Cook for another 2 minutes until fragrant.
4. Stir in the ground cumin, ground coriander, turmeric powder, chili powder, garam masala, and salt. Cook for 1 minute to toast the spices.
5. Add the diced tomatoes (with their juices) to the skillet. Stir well to combine with the onion and spice mixture.
6. Pour in the coconut milk and stir until everything is well combined.
7. Add the cooked lentils to the skillet and stir to coat them with the curry sauce.
8. Let the curry simmer for 5-10 minutes to allow the flavors to meld together.
9. Stir in the chopped spinach leaves and cook until wilted, about 2-3 minutes.
10. Taste and adjust seasoning if needed.
11. Once the lentil spinach curry is ready, remove from heat and garnish with fresh chopped cilantro.
12. Serve hot with cooked rice or naan bread.

Enjoy your delicious Lentil Spinach Curry!

Cauliflower Curry

Ingredients:

- 1 medium head cauliflower, cut into florets
- 2 tablespoons olive oil or coconut oil
- 1 onion, finely chopped
- 3 cloves garlic, minced
- 1 tablespoon grated ginger
- 1 teaspoon ground cumin
- 1 teaspoon ground coriander
- 1 teaspoon turmeric powder
- 1/2 teaspoon chili powder (adjust to taste)
- 1/2 teaspoon garam masala
- Salt to taste
- 1 can (14 oz) diced tomatoes
- 1 can (14 oz) coconut milk
- 2 cups vegetable broth
- Fresh cilantro, chopped (for garnish)
- Cooked rice or naan bread (for serving)

Instructions:

1. Heat the olive oil in a large skillet or pot over medium heat. Add the chopped onion and cook until softened, about 5 minutes.
2. Add the minced garlic and grated ginger to the skillet. Cook for another 2 minutes until fragrant.
3. Stir in the ground cumin, ground coriander, turmeric powder, chili powder, garam masala, and salt. Cook for 1 minute to toast the spices.
4. Add the diced tomatoes (with their juices) to the skillet. Stir well to combine with the onion and spice mixture.
5. Pour in the coconut milk and vegetable broth. Stir until everything is well combined.
6. Add the cauliflower florets to the skillet and stir to coat them with the curry sauce.
7. Bring the mixture to a simmer, then reduce the heat to low. Cover and let it cook for about 15-20 minutes, or until the cauliflower is tender.
8. Taste and adjust seasoning if needed.
9. Once the cauliflower curry is ready, remove from heat and garnish with fresh chopped cilantro.
10. Serve hot with cooked rice or naan bread.

Enjoy your flavorful Cauliflower Curry!

Sweet Potato Curry

Ingredients:

- 2 medium sweet potatoes, peeled and diced
- 2 tablespoons coconut oil or olive oil
- 1 onion, finely chopped
- 3 cloves garlic, minced
- 1 tablespoon grated ginger
- 1 tablespoon curry powder
- 1 teaspoon ground cumin
- 1 teaspoon ground coriander
- 1/2 teaspoon turmeric powder
- 1/4 teaspoon cayenne pepper (optional, for heat)
- 1 can (14 oz) diced tomatoes
- 1 can (14 oz) coconut milk
- 2 cups vegetable broth
- Salt to taste
- Fresh cilantro, chopped (for garnish)
- Cooked rice or naan bread (for serving)

Instructions:

1. Heat the coconut oil or olive oil in a large skillet or pot over medium heat. Add the chopped onion and cook until softened, about 5 minutes.
2. Add the minced garlic and grated ginger to the skillet. Cook for another 2 minutes until fragrant.
3. Stir in the curry powder, ground cumin, ground coriander, turmeric powder, and cayenne pepper (if using). Cook for 1 minute to toast the spices.
4. Add the diced sweet potatoes to the skillet and stir to coat them with the onion and spice mixture.
5. Pour in the diced tomatoes (with their juices), coconut milk, and vegetable broth. Stir until everything is well combined.
6. Bring the mixture to a simmer, then reduce the heat to low. Cover and let it cook for about 20-25 minutes, or until the sweet potatoes are tender.
7. Taste and adjust seasoning with salt as needed.
8. Once the sweet potato curry is ready, remove from heat and garnish with fresh chopped cilantro.
9. Serve hot with cooked rice or naan bread.

Enjoy your delicious Sweet Potato Curry!

Thai Green Curry

Ingredients:

- 2 tablespoons green curry paste (store-bought or homemade)
- 1 can (14 oz) coconut milk
- 1 cup vegetable broth
- 2 tablespoons soy sauce or tamari
- 1 tablespoon coconut sugar or brown sugar
- 1 tablespoon cooking oil
- 1 onion, sliced
- 2 cloves garlic, minced
- 1 tablespoon grated ginger
- 1 green bell pepper, sliced
- 1 medium carrot, sliced
- 1 cup broccoli florets
- 1 cup sliced mushrooms
- 1 block firm tofu, drained and cubed
- Handful of Thai basil leaves (optional, for garnish)
- Cooked rice, for serving

Instructions:

1. Heat the cooking oil in a large skillet or pot over medium heat. Add the sliced onion and cook until softened, about 5 minutes.
2. Add the minced garlic and grated ginger to the skillet. Cook for another 2 minutes until fragrant.
3. Stir in the green curry paste and cook for 1 minute to release its flavors.
4. Pour in the coconut milk, vegetable broth, soy sauce, and coconut sugar. Stir until the ingredients are well combined.
5. Add the sliced bell pepper, carrot, broccoli florets, mushrooms, and tofu to the skillet. Stir to coat the vegetables and tofu with the curry sauce.
6. Bring the mixture to a simmer, then reduce the heat to low. Cover and let it cook for about 10-15 minutes, or until the vegetables are tender and the tofu is heated through.
7. Taste and adjust seasoning with more soy sauce or coconut sugar if needed.
8. Once the Thai Green Curry is ready, remove from heat and garnish with Thai basil leaves.
9. Serve hot with cooked rice.

Enjoy the fragrant and delicious Thai Green Curry!

Coconut Curry with Tofu

Ingredients:

- 1 block (14 oz) firm tofu, drained and pressed
- 2 tablespoons coconut oil or vegetable oil
- 1 onion, diced
- 3 cloves garlic, minced
- 1 tablespoon grated ginger
- 2 tablespoons Thai red curry paste
- 1 can (14 oz) coconut milk
- 1 cup vegetable broth
- 2 tablespoons soy sauce or tamari
- 1 tablespoon coconut sugar or brown sugar
- 1 red bell pepper, sliced
- 1 yellow bell pepper, sliced
- 1 cup broccoli florets
- 1 cup sliced carrots
- Salt to taste
- Fresh cilantro, chopped (for garnish)
- Cooked rice or noodles, for serving

Instructions:

1. Cut the pressed tofu into cubes and set aside.
2. Heat the coconut oil in a large skillet or pot over medium heat. Add the diced onion and cook until softened, about 5 minutes.
3. Add the minced garlic and grated ginger to the skillet. Cook for another 2 minutes until fragrant.
4. Stir in the Thai red curry paste and cook for 1 minute to release its flavors.
5. Pour in the coconut milk, vegetable broth, soy sauce, and coconut sugar. Stir until the ingredients are well combined.
6. Add the sliced bell peppers, broccoli florets, carrots, and tofu cubes to the skillet. Stir to coat them with the curry sauce.
7. Bring the mixture to a simmer, then reduce the heat to low. Cover and let it cook for about 10-15 minutes, or until the vegetables are tender and the tofu is heated through.
8. Taste and adjust seasoning with salt if needed.

9. Once the Coconut Curry with Tofu is ready, remove from heat and garnish with fresh chopped cilantro.
10. Serve hot with cooked rice or noodles.

Enjoy the creamy and flavorful Coconut Curry with Tofu!

Mushroom Curry

Ingredients:

- 2 tablespoons vegetable oil or ghee
- 1 onion, finely chopped
- 3 cloves garlic, minced
- 1 tablespoon grated ginger
- 1 green chili, finely chopped (optional, for heat)
- 1 teaspoon cumin seeds
- 1 teaspoon ground coriander
- 1 teaspoon ground turmeric
- 1/2 teaspoon chili powder (adjust to taste)
- 1/2 teaspoon garam masala
- 1/2 teaspoon paprika
- Salt to taste
- 1 can (14 oz) diced tomatoes
- 1 cup coconut milk
- 1 pound mushrooms, sliced (use your favorite variety)
- Fresh cilantro, chopped (for garnish)
- Cooked rice or naan bread, for serving

Instructions:

1. Heat the vegetable oil or ghee in a large skillet or pot over medium heat. Add the cumin seeds and let them sizzle for a few seconds until fragrant.
2. Add the chopped onion to the skillet and cook until softened and translucent, about 5 minutes.
3. Stir in the minced garlic, grated ginger, and chopped green chili (if using). Cook for another 2 minutes until fragrant.
4. Add the ground coriander, ground turmeric, chili powder, garam masala, paprika, and salt to the skillet. Stir well to combine with the onion mixture.
5. Pour in the diced tomatoes (with their juices) and coconut milk. Stir until everything is well combined.
6. Add the sliced mushrooms to the skillet and stir to coat them with the curry sauce.
7. Bring the mixture to a simmer, then reduce the heat to low. Cover and let it cook for about 10-15 minutes, or until the mushrooms are tender and the sauce has thickened.
8. Taste and adjust seasoning with salt if needed.
9. Once the Mushroom Curry is ready, remove from heat and garnish with fresh chopped cilantro.
10. Serve hot with cooked rice or naan bread.

Enjoy the rich and flavorful Mushroom Curry!

Eggplant Curry

Ingredients:

- 2 medium-sized eggplants, diced
- 3 tablespoons vegetable oil
- 1 onion, finely chopped
- 3 cloves garlic, minced
- 1 tablespoon grated ginger
- 2 tomatoes, chopped
- 1 teaspoon ground cumin
- 1 teaspoon ground coriander
- 1 teaspoon turmeric powder
- 1/2 teaspoon chili powder (adjust to taste)
- 1/2 teaspoon garam masala
- Salt to taste
- 1 cup coconut milk
- Fresh cilantro, chopped (for garnish)
- Cooked rice or naan bread, for serving

Instructions:

1. Heat the vegetable oil in a large skillet or pot over medium heat. Add the chopped onion and cook until softened and translucent, about 5 minutes.
2. Add the minced garlic and grated ginger to the skillet. Cook for another 2 minutes until fragrant.
3. Stir in the chopped tomatoes and cook until they start to soften, about 5 minutes.
4. Add the ground cumin, ground coriander, turmeric powder, chili powder, garam masala, and salt to the skillet. Stir well to combine with the onion and tomato mixture.
5. Add the diced eggplant to the skillet and stir to coat it with the spice mixture.
6. Pour in the coconut milk and stir until everything is well combined.
7. Bring the mixture to a simmer, then reduce the heat to low. Cover and let it cook for about 15-20 minutes, or until the eggplant is tender and cooked through.
8. Taste and adjust seasoning with salt if needed.
9. Once the Eggplant Curry is ready, remove from heat and garnish with fresh chopped cilantro.
10. Serve hot with cooked rice or naan bread.

Enjoy the creamy and flavorful Eggplant Curry!

Red Lentil Curry

Ingredients:

- 1 cup red lentils, rinsed and drained
- 2 tablespoons vegetable oil
- 1 onion, finely chopped
- 3 cloves garlic, minced
- 1 tablespoon grated ginger
- 1 tablespoon curry powder
- 1 teaspoon ground cumin
- 1 teaspoon ground coriander
- 1/2 teaspoon turmeric powder
- 1/4 teaspoon cayenne pepper (adjust to taste)
- Salt to taste
- 1 can (14 oz) diced tomatoes
- 1 can (14 oz) coconut milk
- 2 cups vegetable broth or water
- Fresh cilantro, chopped (for garnish)
- Cooked rice or naan bread, for serving

Instructions:

1. Heat the vegetable oil in a large pot over medium heat. Add the chopped onion and cook until softened and translucent, about 5 minutes.
2. Add the minced garlic and grated ginger to the pot. Cook for another 2 minutes until fragrant.
3. Stir in the curry powder, ground cumin, ground coriander, turmeric powder, cayenne pepper, and salt. Cook for 1 minute to toast the spices.
4. Add the diced tomatoes (with their juices) to the pot. Stir well to combine with the onion and spice mixture.
5. Pour in the coconut milk, vegetable broth or water, and red lentils. Stir until everything is well combined.
6. Bring the mixture to a boil, then reduce the heat to low. Cover and let it simmer for about 20-25 minutes, stirring occasionally, or until the lentils are tender and the curry has thickened.
7. Taste and adjust seasoning with salt if needed.
8. Once the Red Lentil Curry is ready, remove from heat and garnish with fresh chopped cilantro.

9. Serve hot with cooked rice or naan bread.

Enjoy the hearty and flavorful Red Lentil Curry!

Butternut Squash Curry

Ingredients:

- 1 medium butternut squash, peeled, seeded, and diced
- 2 tablespoons vegetable oil or coconut oil
- 1 onion, finely chopped
- 3 cloves garlic, minced
- 1 tablespoon grated ginger
- 2 tablespoons curry powder
- 1 teaspoon ground cumin
- 1 teaspoon ground coriander
- 1/2 teaspoon turmeric powder
- 1/4 teaspoon cayenne pepper (optional, for heat)
- Salt to taste
- 1 can (14 oz) diced tomatoes
- 1 can (14 oz) coconut milk
- 2 cups vegetable broth or water
- Fresh cilantro, chopped (for garnish)
- Cooked rice or naan bread, for serving

Instructions:

1. Heat the vegetable oil or coconut oil in a large pot over medium heat. Add the chopped onion and cook until softened and translucent, about 5 minutes.
2. Add the minced garlic and grated ginger to the pot. Cook for another 2 minutes until fragrant.
3. Stir in the curry powder, ground cumin, ground coriander, turmeric powder, cayenne pepper (if using), and salt. Cook for 1 minute to toast the spices.
4. Add the diced butternut squash to the pot. Stir well to coat it with the onion and spice mixture.
5. Pour in the diced tomatoes (with their juices), coconut milk, and vegetable broth or water. Stir until everything is well combined.
6. Bring the mixture to a boil, then reduce the heat to low. Cover and let it simmer for about 20-25 minutes, stirring occasionally, or until the butternut squash is tender.
7. Taste and adjust seasoning with salt if needed.
8. Once the Butternut Squash Curry is ready, remove from heat and garnish with fresh chopped cilantro.
9. Serve hot with cooked rice or naan bread.

Enjoy the creamy and flavorful Butternut Squash Curry!

Potato Curry

Ingredients:

- 4 medium potatoes, peeled and diced
- 2 tablespoons vegetable oil
- 1 onion, finely chopped
- 3 cloves garlic, minced
- 1 tablespoon grated ginger
- 2 tomatoes, chopped
- 1 tablespoon curry powder
- 1 teaspoon ground cumin
- 1 teaspoon ground coriander
- 1/2 teaspoon turmeric powder
- 1/4 teaspoon cayenne pepper (optional, for heat)
- Salt to taste
- 1 cup vegetable broth or water
- Fresh cilantro, chopped (for garnish)
- Cooked rice or naan bread, for serving

Instructions:

1. Heat the vegetable oil in a large skillet or pot over medium heat. Add the chopped onion and cook until softened and translucent, about 5 minutes.
2. Add the minced garlic and grated ginger to the skillet. Cook for another 2 minutes until fragrant.
3. Stir in the chopped tomatoes and cook until they start to soften, about 5 minutes.
4. Add the curry powder, ground cumin, ground coriander, turmeric powder, cayenne pepper (if using), and salt to the skillet. Stir well to combine with the onion and tomato mixture.
5. Add the diced potatoes to the skillet and stir to coat them with the spice mixture.
6. Pour in the vegetable broth or water. Stir until everything is well combined.
7. Bring the mixture to a boil, then reduce the heat to low. Cover and let it simmer for about 20-25 minutes, or until the potatoes are tender and cooked through, stirring occasionally.
8. Taste and adjust seasoning with salt if needed.
9. Once the Potato Curry is ready, remove from heat and garnish with fresh chopped cilantro.
10. Serve hot with cooked rice or naan bread.

Enjoy the delicious and comforting Potato Curry!

Vegan Butter Chicken Curry

Ingredients:

- 1 block (14 oz) firm tofu, drained and cubed (or 2 cups cooked chickpeas)
- 2 tablespoons vegetable oil
- 1 onion, finely chopped
- 3 cloves garlic, minced
- 1 tablespoon grated ginger
- 2 tomatoes, chopped
- 1/4 cup tomato paste
- 1/4 cup vegan butter
- 1 tablespoon curry powder
- 1 teaspoon ground cumin
- 1 teaspoon ground coriander
- 1/2 teaspoon turmeric powder
- 1/4 teaspoon cayenne pepper (adjust to taste)
- 1/2 cup coconut cream
- 1/2 cup vegetable broth
- Salt to taste
- Fresh cilantro, chopped (for garnish)
- Cooked rice or naan bread, for serving

Instructions:

1. Heat 1 tablespoon of vegetable oil in a large skillet over medium heat. Add the cubed tofu (or cooked chickpeas) and cook until golden brown on all sides, about 8-10 minutes. Remove the tofu from the skillet and set aside.
2. In the same skillet, heat the remaining 1 tablespoon of vegetable oil. Add the chopped onion and cook until softened and translucent, about 5 minutes.
3. Add the minced garlic and grated ginger to the skillet. Cook for another 2 minutes until fragrant.
4. Stir in the chopped tomatoes and tomato paste. Cook until the tomatoes break down and the mixture thickens, about 8-10 minutes.
5. Add the vegan butter to the skillet and stir until melted.
6. Stir in the curry powder, ground cumin, ground coriander, turmeric powder, and cayenne pepper. Cook for 1 minute to toast the spices.
7. Add the coconut cream and vegetable broth to the skillet. Stir until everything is well combined.

8. Return the cooked tofu (or chickpeas) to the skillet. Stir to coat them with the curry sauce.
9. Bring the mixture to a simmer, then reduce the heat to low. Cover and let it simmer for about 10-15 minutes, stirring occasionally.
10. Taste and adjust seasoning with salt if needed.
11. Once the Vegan Butter Chicken Curry is ready, remove from heat and garnish with fresh chopped cilantro.
12. Serve hot with cooked rice or naan bread.

Enjoy the creamy and flavorful Vegan Butter Chicken Curry!

Jackfruit Curry

Ingredients:

- 2 cans (20 oz each) young green jackfruit in water or brine, drained and rinsed
- 2 tablespoons vegetable oil
- 1 onion, finely chopped
- 3 cloves garlic, minced
- 1 tablespoon grated ginger
- 2 tomatoes, chopped
- 1 tablespoon curry powder
- 1 teaspoon ground cumin
- 1 teaspoon ground coriander
- 1/2 teaspoon turmeric powder
- 1/4 teaspoon cayenne pepper (adjust to taste)
- 1 can (14 oz) coconut milk
- 1 cup vegetable broth
- Salt to taste
- Fresh cilantro, chopped (for garnish)
- Cooked rice or naan bread, for serving

Instructions:

1. Heat the vegetable oil in a large skillet or pot over medium heat. Add the chopped onion and cook until softened and translucent, about 5 minutes.
2. Add the minced garlic and grated ginger to the skillet. Cook for another 2 minutes until fragrant.
3. Stir in the chopped tomatoes and cook until they start to soften, about 5 minutes.
4. Add the curry powder, ground cumin, ground coriander, turmeric powder, and cayenne pepper to the skillet. Cook for 1 minute to toast the spices.
5. Add the drained and rinsed jackfruit to the skillet. Stir well to coat it with the onion and spice mixture.
6. Pour in the coconut milk and vegetable broth. Stir until everything is well combined.
7. Bring the mixture to a simmer, then reduce the heat to low. Cover and let it cook for about 20-25 minutes, stirring occasionally, or until the jackfruit is tender.
8. Taste and adjust seasoning with salt if needed.
9. Once the Jackfruit Curry is ready, remove from heat and garnish with fresh chopped cilantro.
10. Serve hot with cooked rice or naan bread.

Enjoy the aromatic and flavorful Jackfruit Curry!

Black Bean Curry

Ingredients:

- 2 cans (15 oz each) black beans, drained and rinsed
- 2 tablespoons vegetable oil
- 1 onion, finely chopped
- 3 cloves garlic, minced
- 1 tablespoon grated ginger
- 2 tomatoes, chopped
- 1 tablespoon curry powder
- 1 teaspoon ground cumin
- 1 teaspoon ground coriander
- 1/2 teaspoon turmeric powder
- 1/4 teaspoon cayenne pepper (adjust to taste)
- Salt to taste
- 1 can (14 oz) coconut milk
- 1 cup vegetable broth
- Fresh cilantro, chopped (for garnish)
- Cooked rice or naan bread, for serving

Instructions:

1. Heat the vegetable oil in a large skillet or pot over medium heat. Add the chopped onion and cook until softened and translucent, about 5 minutes.
2. Add the minced garlic and grated ginger to the skillet. Cook for another 2 minutes until fragrant.
3. Stir in the chopped tomatoes and cook until they start to soften, about 5 minutes.
4. Add the curry powder, ground cumin, ground coriander, turmeric powder, and cayenne pepper to the skillet. Cook for 1 minute to toast the spices.
5. Add the drained and rinsed black beans to the skillet. Stir well to coat them with the onion and spice mixture.
6. Pour in the coconut milk and vegetable broth. Stir until everything is well combined.
7. Bring the mixture to a simmer, then reduce the heat to low. Cover and let it cook for about 15-20 minutes, stirring occasionally, to allow the flavors to meld together and the sauce to thicken.
8. Taste and adjust seasoning with salt if needed.
9. Once the Black Bean Curry is ready, remove from heat and garnish with fresh chopped cilantro.
10. Serve hot with cooked rice or naan bread.

Enjoy the delicious and satisfying Black Bean Curry!

Pumpkin Curry

Ingredients:

- 2 cups pumpkin, peeled and diced
- 2 tablespoons vegetable oil
- 1 onion, finely chopped
- 3 cloves garlic, minced
- 1 tablespoon grated ginger
- 2 tomatoes, chopped
- 1 tablespoon curry powder
- 1 teaspoon ground cumin
- 1 teaspoon ground coriander
- 1/2 teaspoon turmeric powder
- 1/4 teaspoon cayenne pepper (adjust to taste)
- Salt to taste
- 1 can (14 oz) coconut milk
- 1 cup vegetable broth
- Fresh cilantro, chopped (for garnish)
- Cooked rice or naan bread, for serving

Instructions:

1. Heat the vegetable oil in a large skillet or pot over medium heat. Add the chopped onion and cook until softened and translucent, about 5 minutes.
2. Add the minced garlic and grated ginger to the skillet. Cook for another 2 minutes until fragrant.
3. Stir in the chopped tomatoes and cook until they start to soften, about 5 minutes.
4. Add the diced pumpkin to the skillet. Stir well to combine with the onion and tomato mixture.
5. Add the curry powder, ground cumin, ground coriander, turmeric powder, and cayenne pepper to the skillet. Cook for 1 minute to toast the spices.
6. Pour in the coconut milk and vegetable broth. Stir until everything is well combined.
7. Bring the mixture to a simmer, then reduce the heat to low. Cover and let it cook for about 20-25 minutes, stirring occasionally, or until the pumpkin is tender.
8. Taste and adjust seasoning with salt if needed.
9. Once the Pumpkin Curry is ready, remove from heat and garnish with fresh chopped cilantro.

10. Serve hot with cooked rice or naan bread.

Enjoy the delicious and warming Pumpkin Curry!

Pea and Potato Curry

Ingredients:

- 2 tablespoons vegetable oil
- 1 onion, finely chopped
- 3 cloves garlic, minced
- 1 tablespoon grated ginger
- 2 tomatoes, chopped
- 2 potatoes, peeled and diced
- 1 cup peas (fresh or frozen)
- 1 tablespoon curry powder
- 1 teaspoon ground cumin
- 1 teaspoon ground coriander
- 1/2 teaspoon turmeric powder
- 1/4 teaspoon cayenne pepper (adjust to taste)
- Salt to taste
- 1 can (14 oz) coconut milk
- 1 cup vegetable broth
- Fresh cilantro, chopped (for garnish)
- Cooked rice or naan bread, for serving

Instructions:

1. Heat the vegetable oil in a large skillet or pot over medium heat. Add the chopped onion and cook until softened and translucent, about 5 minutes.
2. Add the minced garlic and grated ginger to the skillet. Cook for another 2 minutes until fragrant.
3. Stir in the chopped tomatoes and cook until they start to soften, about 5 minutes.
4. Add the diced potatoes to the skillet. Stir well to combine with the onion and tomato mixture.
5. Add the curry powder, ground cumin, ground coriander, turmeric powder, and cayenne pepper to the skillet. Cook for 1 minute to toast the spices.
6. Add the peas to the skillet. Stir well to combine.
7. Pour in the coconut milk and vegetable broth. Stir until everything is well combined.
8. Bring the mixture to a simmer, then reduce the heat to low. Cover and let it cook for about 20-25 minutes, stirring occasionally, or until the potatoes are tender.
9. Taste and adjust seasoning with salt if needed.

10. Once the Pea and Potato Curry is ready, remove from heat and garnish with fresh chopped cilantro.
11. Serve hot with cooked rice or naan bread.

Enjoy the flavorful and satisfying Pea and Potato Curry!

Okra Curry

Ingredients:

- 2 cups fresh okra, trimmed and cut into bite-sized pieces
- 2 tablespoons vegetable oil
- 1 onion, finely chopped
- 3 cloves garlic, minced
- 1 tablespoon grated ginger
- 2 tomatoes, chopped
- 1 tablespoon curry powder
- 1 teaspoon ground cumin
- 1 teaspoon ground coriander
- 1/2 teaspoon turmeric powder
- 1/4 teaspoon cayenne pepper (adjust to taste)
- Salt to taste
- 1 can (14 oz) coconut milk
- 1 cup vegetable broth
- Fresh cilantro, chopped (for garnish)
- Cooked rice or naan bread, for serving

Instructions:

1. Heat the vegetable oil in a large skillet or pot over medium heat. Add the chopped onion and cook until softened and translucent, about 5 minutes.
2. Add the minced garlic and grated ginger to the skillet. Cook for another 2 minutes until fragrant.
3. Stir in the chopped tomatoes and cook until they start to soften, about 5 minutes.
4. Add the okra pieces to the skillet. Stir well to combine with the onion and tomato mixture.
5. Add the curry powder, ground cumin, ground coriander, turmeric powder, and cayenne pepper to the skillet. Cook for 1 minute to toast the spices.
6. Pour in the coconut milk and vegetable broth. Stir until everything is well combined.
7. Bring the mixture to a simmer, then reduce the heat to low. Cover and let it cook for about 15-20 minutes, stirring occasionally, or until the okra is tender.
8. Taste and adjust seasoning with salt if needed.
9. Once the Okra Curry is ready, remove from heat and garnish with fresh chopped cilantro.
10. Serve hot with cooked rice or naan bread.

Enjoy the aromatic and flavorful Okra Curry!

Spinach and Potato Curry

Ingredients:

- 2 tablespoons vegetable oil
- 1 onion, finely chopped
- 3 cloves garlic, minced
- 1 tablespoon grated ginger
- 2 tomatoes, chopped
- 2 potatoes, peeled and diced
- 4 cups fresh spinach leaves, chopped
- 1 tablespoon curry powder
- 1 teaspoon ground cumin
- 1 teaspoon ground coriander
- 1/2 teaspoon turmeric powder
- 1/4 teaspoon cayenne pepper (adjust to taste)
- Salt to taste
- 1 can (14 oz) coconut milk
- 1 cup vegetable broth
- Fresh cilantro, chopped (for garnish)
- Cooked rice or naan bread, for serving

Instructions:

1. Heat the vegetable oil in a large skillet or pot over medium heat. Add the chopped onion and cook until softened and translucent, about 5 minutes.
2. Add the minced garlic and grated ginger to the skillet. Cook for another 2 minutes until fragrant.
3. Stir in the chopped tomatoes and cook until they start to soften, about 5 minutes.
4. Add the diced potatoes to the skillet. Stir well to combine with the onion and tomato mixture.
5. Add the curry powder, ground cumin, ground coriander, turmeric powder, and cayenne pepper to the skillet. Cook for 1 minute to toast the spices.
6. Add the chopped spinach leaves to the skillet. Stir well to combine.
7. Pour in the coconut milk and vegetable broth. Stir until everything is well combined.
8. Bring the mixture to a simmer, then reduce the heat to low. Cover and let it cook for about 15-20 minutes, stirring occasionally, or until the potatoes are tender.
9. Taste and adjust seasoning with salt if needed.
10. Once the Spinach and Potato Curry is ready, remove from heat and garnish with fresh chopped cilantro.
11. Serve hot with cooked rice or naan bread.

Enjoy the nutritious and delicious Spinach and Potato Curry!

Masoor Dal Curry

Ingredients:

- 1 cup masoor dal (red lentils), rinsed and drained
- 3 cups water
- 2 tablespoons vegetable oil
- 1 onion, finely chopped
- 3 cloves garlic, minced
- 1 tablespoon grated ginger
- 2 tomatoes, chopped
- 1 teaspoon ground turmeric
- 1 teaspoon ground cumin
- 1 teaspoon ground coriander
- 1/2 teaspoon red chili powder (adjust to taste)
- Salt to taste
- Fresh cilantro, chopped (for garnish)
- Cooked rice or naan bread, for serving

Instructions:

1. In a large pot, combine the rinsed masoor dal and water. Bring to a boil over medium-high heat, then reduce the heat to low and let it simmer for about 20-25 minutes, or until the lentils are soft and cooked through. Stir occasionally and skim off any foam that forms on the surface.
2. In a separate skillet or pan, heat the vegetable oil over medium heat. Add the chopped onion and cook until softened and translucent, about 5 minutes.
3. Add the minced garlic and grated ginger to the skillet. Cook for another 2 minutes until fragrant.
4. Stir in the chopped tomatoes and cook until they start to soften, about 5 minutes.
5. Add the ground turmeric, ground cumin, ground coriander, and red chili powder to the skillet. Cook for 1 minute to toast the spices.
6. Add the cooked masoor dal to the skillet, along with any remaining cooking water. Stir well to combine with the onion and tomato mixture.
7. Season with salt to taste and let the curry simmer for another 5-10 minutes to allow the flavors to meld together.
8. Taste and adjust seasoning if needed.
9. Once the Masoor Dal Curry is ready, remove from heat and garnish with fresh chopped cilantro.
10. Serve hot with cooked rice or naan bread.

Enjoy the hearty and flavorful Masoor Dal Curry!

Chickpea and Spinach Curry

Ingredients:

- 2 tablespoons vegetable oil
- 1 onion, finely chopped
- 3 cloves garlic, minced
- 1 tablespoon grated ginger
- 2 tomatoes, chopped
- 2 cups cooked chickpeas (or 2 cans, drained and rinsed)
- 4 cups fresh spinach leaves, chopped
- 1 tablespoon curry powder
- 1 teaspoon ground cumin
- 1 teaspoon ground coriander
- 1/2 teaspoon turmeric powder
- 1/4 teaspoon cayenne pepper (adjust to taste)
- Salt to taste
- 1 can (14 oz) coconut milk
- Fresh cilantro, chopped (for garnish)
- Cooked rice or naan bread, for serving

Instructions:

1. Heat the vegetable oil in a large skillet or pot over medium heat. Add the chopped onion and cook until softened and translucent, about 5 minutes.
2. Add the minced garlic and grated ginger to the skillet. Cook for another 2 minutes until fragrant.
3. Stir in the chopped tomatoes and cook until they start to soften, about 5 minutes.
4. Add the cooked chickpeas to the skillet. Stir well to combine with the onion and tomato mixture.
5. Add the chopped spinach leaves to the skillet. Stir well to combine.
6. Add the curry powder, ground cumin, ground coriander, turmeric powder, and cayenne pepper to the skillet. Cook for 1 minute to toast the spices.
7. Pour in the coconut milk. Stir until everything is well combined.
8. Bring the mixture to a simmer, then reduce the heat to low. Cover and let it cook for about 10-15 minutes, stirring occasionally, or until the spinach is wilted and the flavors are blended.
9. Taste and adjust seasoning with salt if needed.

10. Once the Chickpea and Spinach Curry is ready, remove from heat and garnish with fresh chopped cilantro.
11. Serve hot with cooked rice or naan bread.

Enjoy the delicious and nutritious Chickpea and Spinach Curry!

Tofu Tikka Masala

Ingredients:

For the Tofu Marinade:

- 1 block (14 oz) firm tofu, pressed and cubed
- 1/4 cup dairy-free yogurt
- 2 tablespoons lemon juice
- 1 tablespoon grated ginger
- 2 cloves garlic, minced
- 1 teaspoon ground cumin
- 1 teaspoon ground coriander
- 1/2 teaspoon paprika
- 1/2 teaspoon turmeric
- Salt to taste

For the Tikka Masala Sauce:

- 2 tablespoons vegetable oil
- 1 onion, finely chopped
- 3 cloves garlic, minced
- 1 tablespoon grated ginger
- 2 tomatoes, chopped
- 1 tablespoon tomato paste
- 1 teaspoon ground cumin
- 1 teaspoon ground coriander
- 1 teaspoon garam masala
- 1/2 teaspoon paprika
- 1/4 teaspoon cayenne pepper (adjust to taste)
- 1 cup coconut milk
- Salt to taste
- Fresh cilantro, chopped (for garnish)
- Cooked rice or naan bread, for serving

Instructions:

1. In a bowl, combine all the ingredients for the tofu marinade: dairy-free yogurt, lemon juice, grated ginger, minced garlic, ground cumin, ground coriander, paprika, turmeric, and salt. Mix well.
2. Add the cubed tofu to the marinade and toss until well coated. Cover and refrigerate for at least 30 minutes, or up to overnight.

3. Preheat the oven to 400°F (200°C). Place the marinated tofu cubes on a baking sheet lined with parchment paper. Bake for 20-25 minutes, or until the tofu is golden brown and slightly crispy.
4. While the tofu is baking, prepare the Tikka Masala sauce. Heat the vegetable oil in a large skillet or pot over medium heat. Add the chopped onion and cook until softened and translucent, about 5 minutes.
5. Add the minced garlic and grated ginger to the skillet. Cook for another 2 minutes until fragrant.
6. Stir in the chopped tomatoes and cook until they start to soften, about 5 minutes.
7. Add the tomato paste, ground cumin, ground coriander, garam masala, paprika, and cayenne pepper to the skillet. Cook for 1 minute to toast the spices.
8. Pour in the coconut milk and stir until everything is well combined. Bring the mixture to a simmer, then reduce the heat to low.
9. Once the tofu is baked, add it to the skillet with the Tikka Masala sauce. Stir gently to coat the tofu with the sauce. Let it simmer for another 5-10 minutes to allow the flavors to meld together.
10. Taste and adjust seasoning with salt if needed.
11. Once the Tofu Tikka Masala is ready, remove from heat and garnish with fresh chopped cilantro.
12. Serve hot with cooked rice or naan bread.

Enjoy the flavorful and aromatic Tofu Tikka Masala!

Mushroom and Pea Curry

Ingredients:

- 2 tablespoons vegetable oil
- 1 onion, finely chopped
- 3 cloves garlic, minced
- 1 tablespoon grated ginger
- 2 tomatoes, chopped
- 8 oz mushrooms, sliced
- 1 cup peas (fresh or frozen)
- 1 tablespoon curry powder
- 1 teaspoon ground cumin
- 1 teaspoon ground coriander
- 1/2 teaspoon turmeric powder
- 1/4 teaspoon cayenne pepper (adjust to taste)
- Salt to taste
- 1 can (14 oz) coconut milk
- Fresh cilantro, chopped (for garnish)
- Cooked rice or naan bread, for serving

Instructions:

1. Heat the vegetable oil in a large skillet or pot over medium heat. Add the chopped onion and cook until softened and translucent, about 5 minutes.
2. Add the minced garlic and grated ginger to the skillet. Cook for another 2 minutes until fragrant.
3. Stir in the chopped tomatoes and cook until they start to soften, about 5 minutes.
4. Add the sliced mushrooms to the skillet. Cook until they release their moisture and start to brown, about 5-7 minutes.
5. Add the peas to the skillet. Stir well to combine.
6. Add the curry powder, ground cumin, ground coriander, turmeric powder, and cayenne pepper to the skillet. Cook for 1 minute to toast the spices.
7. Pour in the coconut milk. Stir until everything is well combined.
8. Bring the mixture to a simmer, then reduce the heat to low. Cover and let it cook for about 10-15 minutes, stirring occasionally, or until the mushrooms and peas are tender.
9. Taste and adjust seasoning with salt if needed.

10. Once the Mushroom and Pea Curry is ready, remove from heat and garnish with fresh chopped cilantro.
11. Serve hot with cooked rice or naan bread.

Enjoy the delicious and comforting Mushroom and Pea Curry!

Cashew Curry

Ingredients:

- 1 cup raw cashews
- 2 tablespoons vegetable oil
- 1 onion, finely chopped
- 3 cloves garlic, minced
- 1 tablespoon grated ginger
- 2 tomatoes, chopped
- 1 tablespoon curry powder
- 1 teaspoon ground cumin
- 1 teaspoon ground coriander
- 1/2 teaspoon turmeric powder
- 1/4 teaspoon cayenne pepper (adjust to taste)
- Salt to taste
- 1 can (14 oz) coconut milk
- 1 cup vegetable broth
- Fresh cilantro, chopped (for garnish)
- Cooked rice or naan bread, for serving

Instructions:

1. Place the raw cashews in a bowl and cover with water. Let them soak for at least 2 hours, or overnight. Drain and rinse the cashews before using.
2. In a blender or food processor, combine the soaked cashews with 1 cup of vegetable broth. Blend until smooth and creamy. Set aside.
3. Heat the vegetable oil in a large skillet or pot over medium heat. Add the chopped onion and cook until softened and translucent, about 5 minutes.
4. Add the minced garlic and grated ginger to the skillet. Cook for another 2 minutes until fragrant.
5. Stir in the chopped tomatoes and cook until they start to soften, about 5 minutes.
6. Add the curry powder, ground cumin, ground coriander, turmeric powder, and cayenne pepper to the skillet. Cook for 1 minute to toast the spices.
7. Pour in the cashew cream mixture and coconut milk. Stir until everything is well combined.
8. Bring the mixture to a simmer, then reduce the heat to low. Let it cook for about 10-15 minutes, stirring occasionally, to allow the flavors to meld together and the sauce to thicken.
9. Taste and adjust seasoning with salt if needed.
10. Once the Cashew Curry is ready, remove from heat and garnish with fresh chopped cilantro.
11. Serve hot with cooked rice or naan bread.

Enjoy the creamy and luxurious Cashew Curry!

Zucchini Curry

Ingredients:

- 2 tablespoons vegetable oil
- 1 onion, finely chopped
- 3 cloves garlic, minced
- 1 tablespoon grated ginger
- 2 tomatoes, chopped
- 2 zucchinis, sliced
- 1 can (14 oz) chickpeas, drained and rinsed
- 1 tablespoon curry powder
- 1 teaspoon ground cumin
- 1 teaspoon ground coriander
- 1/2 teaspoon turmeric powder
- 1/4 teaspoon cayenne pepper (adjust to taste)
- Salt to taste
- 1 can (14 oz) coconut milk
- Fresh cilantro, chopped (for garnish)
- Cooked rice or naan bread, for serving

Instructions:

1. Heat the vegetable oil in a large skillet or pot over medium heat. Add the chopped onion and cook until softened and translucent, about 5 minutes.
2. Add the minced garlic and grated ginger to the skillet. Cook for another 2 minutes until fragrant.
3. Stir in the chopped tomatoes and cook until they start to soften, about 5 minutes.
4. Add the sliced zucchinis to the skillet. Cook until they are slightly softened, about 5 minutes.
5. Add the drained chickpeas to the skillet. Stir well to combine.
6. Add the curry powder, ground cumin, ground coriander, turmeric powder, and cayenne pepper to the skillet. Cook for 1 minute to toast the spices.
7. Pour in the coconut milk. Stir until everything is well combined.
8. Bring the mixture to a simmer, then reduce the heat to low. Cover and let it cook for about 10-15 minutes, stirring occasionally, or until the zucchinis are tender.
9. Taste and adjust seasoning with salt if needed.
10. Once the Zucchini Curry is ready, remove from heat and garnish with fresh chopped cilantro.

11. Serve hot with cooked rice or naan bread.

Enjoy the delicious and nutritious Zucchini Curry!

Mixed Vegetable Curry

Ingredients:

- 2 tablespoons vegetable oil
- 1 onion, finely chopped
- 3 cloves garlic, minced
- 1 tablespoon grated ginger
- 2 tomatoes, chopped
- Assorted vegetables (such as carrots, bell peppers, cauliflower, broccoli, peas, etc.), chopped or sliced
- 1 can (14 oz) chickpeas or any other beans of your choice, drained and rinsed (optional)
- 1 tablespoon curry powder
- 1 teaspoon ground cumin
- 1 teaspoon ground coriander
- 1/2 teaspoon turmeric powder
- 1/4 teaspoon cayenne pepper (adjust to taste)
- Salt to taste
- 1 can (14 oz) coconut milk or 1 cup vegetable broth
- Fresh cilantro, chopped (for garnish)
- Cooked rice or naan bread, for serving

Instructions:

1. Heat the vegetable oil in a large skillet or pot over medium heat. Add the chopped onion and cook until softened and translucent, about 5 minutes.
2. Add the minced garlic and grated ginger to the skillet. Cook for another 2 minutes until fragrant.
3. Stir in the chopped tomatoes and cook until they start to soften, about 5 minutes.
4. Add the assorted vegetables to the skillet. If using harder vegetables like carrots or cauliflower, you may want to add them first and cook for a few minutes before adding quicker-cooking vegetables like bell peppers or peas.
5. Add the drained chickpeas or beans to the skillet, if using.
6. Add the curry powder, ground cumin, ground coriander, turmeric powder, and cayenne pepper to the skillet. Cook for 1 minute to toast the spices.
7. Pour in the coconut milk or vegetable broth. Stir until everything is well combined.
8. Bring the mixture to a simmer, then reduce the heat to low. Cover and let it cook for about 10-15 minutes, stirring occasionally, or until the vegetables are tender.
9. Taste and adjust seasoning with salt if needed.
10. Once the Mixed Vegetable Curry is ready, remove from heat and garnish with fresh chopped cilantro.
11. Serve hot with cooked rice or naan bread.

Enjoy the flavorful and nutritious Mixed Vegetable Curry!

Kidney Bean Curry

Ingredients:

- 2 tablespoons vegetable oil
- 1 onion, finely chopped
- 3 cloves garlic, minced
- 1 tablespoon grated ginger
- 2 tomatoes, chopped
- 2 cans (15 oz each) kidney beans, drained and rinsed
- 1 tablespoon curry powder
- 1 teaspoon ground cumin
- 1 teaspoon ground coriander
- 1/2 teaspoon turmeric powder
- 1/4 teaspoon cayenne pepper (adjust to taste)
- Salt to taste
- 1 cup vegetable broth or water
- Fresh cilantro, chopped (for garnish)
- Cooked rice or naan bread, for serving

Instructions:

1. Heat the vegetable oil in a large skillet or pot over medium heat. Add the chopped onion and cook until softened and translucent, about 5 minutes.
2. Add the minced garlic and grated ginger to the skillet. Cook for another 2 minutes until fragrant.
3. Stir in the chopped tomatoes and cook until they start to soften, about 5 minutes.
4. Add the drained and rinsed kidney beans to the skillet. Stir well to combine with the onion and tomato mixture.
5. Add the curry powder, ground cumin, ground coriander, turmeric powder, and cayenne pepper to the skillet. Cook for 1 minute to toast the spices.
6. Pour in the vegetable broth or water. Stir until everything is well combined.
7. Bring the mixture to a simmer, then reduce the heat to low. Cover and let it cook for about 15-20 minutes, stirring occasionally, to allow the flavors to meld together and the sauce to thicken.
8. Taste and adjust seasoning with salt if needed.
9. Once the Kidney Bean Curry is ready, remove from heat and garnish with fresh chopped cilantro.
10. Serve hot with cooked rice or naan bread.

Enjoy the delicious and satisfying Kidney Bean Curry!

Vegan Korma

Ingredients:

- 2 tablespoons vegetable oil
- 1 onion, finely chopped
- 3 cloves garlic, minced
- 1 tablespoon grated ginger
- 2 tomatoes, chopped
- Assorted vegetables (such as carrots, potatoes, cauliflower, peas, etc.), chopped or sliced
- 1 cup cashews, soaked in water for 2 hours and drained
- 1 can (14 oz) coconut milk
- 1 tablespoon curry powder
- 1 teaspoon ground cumin
- 1 teaspoon ground coriander
- 1/2 teaspoon turmeric powder
- 1/4 teaspoon cayenne pepper (adjust to taste)
- Salt to taste
- Fresh cilantro, chopped (for garnish)
- Cooked rice or naan bread, for serving

Instructions:

1. Heat the vegetable oil in a large skillet or pot over medium heat. Add the chopped onion and cook until softened and translucent, about 5 minutes.
2. Add the minced garlic and grated ginger to the skillet. Cook for another 2 minutes until fragrant.
3. Stir in the chopped tomatoes and cook until they start to soften, about 5 minutes.
4. Add the assorted vegetables to the skillet. Cook until they are slightly softened, about 5-7 minutes.
5. In a blender or food processor, combine the soaked cashews and coconut milk. Blend until smooth and creamy.
6. Add the cashew-coconut mixture to the skillet. Stir until everything is well combined.
7. Add the curry powder, ground cumin, ground coriander, turmeric powder, and cayenne pepper to the skillet. Cook for 1 minute to toast the spices.
8. Bring the mixture to a simmer, then reduce the heat to low. Cover and let it cook for about 10-15 minutes, stirring occasionally, or until the vegetables are tender.

9. Taste and adjust seasoning with salt if needed.
10. Once the Vegan Korma is ready, remove from heat and garnish with fresh chopped cilantro.
11. Serve hot with cooked rice or naan bread.

Enjoy the creamy and flavorful Vegan Korma!

Spicy Tomato Curry

Ingredients:

- 2 tablespoons vegetable oil
- 1 onion, finely chopped
- 3 cloves garlic, minced
- 1 tablespoon grated ginger
- 4 tomatoes, chopped
- 1 green chili, chopped (adjust to taste)
- 1 teaspoon ground cumin
- 1 teaspoon ground coriander
- 1/2 teaspoon turmeric powder
- 1/4 teaspoon cayenne pepper (adjust to taste)
- Salt to taste
- 1 cup vegetable broth or water
- Fresh cilantro, chopped (for garnish)
- Cooked rice or naan bread, for serving

Instructions:

1. Heat the vegetable oil in a large skillet or pot over medium heat. Add the chopped onion and cook until softened and translucent, about 5 minutes.
2. Add the minced garlic, grated ginger, and chopped green chili to the skillet. Cook for another 2 minutes until fragrant.
3. Stir in the chopped tomatoes and cook until they start to soften and release their juices, about 5 minutes.
4. Add the ground cumin, ground coriander, turmeric powder, and cayenne pepper to the skillet. Cook for 1 minute to toast the spices.
5. Pour in the vegetable broth or water. Stir until everything is well combined.
6. Bring the mixture to a simmer, then reduce the heat to low. Cover and let it cook for about 15-20 minutes, stirring occasionally, to allow the flavors to meld together and the sauce to thicken.
7. Taste and adjust seasoning with salt if needed.
8. Once the Spicy Tomato Curry is ready, remove from heat and garnish with fresh chopped cilantro.
9. Serve hot with cooked rice or naan bread.

Enjoy the tangy and spicy Spicy Tomato Curry! Adjust the spiciness according to your preference by adding more or less cayenne pepper.

Carrot and Lentil Curry

Ingredients:

- 2 tablespoons vegetable oil
- 1 onion, finely chopped
- 3 cloves garlic, minced
- 1 tablespoon grated ginger
- 2 carrots, diced
- 1 cup dried red lentils, rinsed and drained
- 2 tomatoes, chopped
- 1 tablespoon curry powder
- 1 teaspoon ground cumin
- 1 teaspoon ground coriander
- 1/2 teaspoon turmeric powder
- 1/4 teaspoon cayenne pepper (adjust to taste)
- Salt to taste
- 3 cups vegetable broth or water
- Fresh cilantro, chopped (for garnish)
- Cooked rice or naan bread, for serving

Instructions:

1. Heat the vegetable oil in a large skillet or pot over medium heat. Add the chopped onion and cook until softened and translucent, about 5 minutes.
2. Add the minced garlic and grated ginger to the skillet. Cook for another 2 minutes until fragrant.
3. Stir in the diced carrots and cook for about 5 minutes until they start to soften.
4. Add the rinsed red lentils to the skillet. Stir well to combine with the onion and carrot mixture.
5. Add the chopped tomatoes to the skillet. Stir well.
6. Add the curry powder, ground cumin, ground coriander, turmeric powder, and cayenne pepper to the skillet. Cook for 1 minute to toast the spices.
7. Pour in the vegetable broth or water. Stir until everything is well combined.
8. Bring the mixture to a boil, then reduce the heat to low. Cover and let it simmer for about 20-25 minutes, stirring occasionally, or until the lentils are cooked and the carrots are tender.
9. Taste and adjust seasoning with salt if needed.
10. Once the Carrot and Lentil Curry is ready, remove from heat and garnish with fresh chopped cilantro.
11. Serve hot with cooked rice or naan bread.

Enjoy the hearty and flavorful Carrot and Lentil Curry! Adjust the consistency by adding more broth or water if desired.

Tempeh Curry

Ingredients:

- 2 tablespoons vegetable oil
- 1 onion, finely chopped
- 3 cloves garlic, minced
- 1 tablespoon grated ginger
- 2 tomatoes, chopped
- 1 block (8 oz) tempeh, cubed
- Assorted vegetables (such as bell peppers, carrots, potatoes, peas, etc.), chopped or sliced
- 1 can (14 oz) coconut milk
- 1 tablespoon curry powder
- 1 teaspoon ground cumin
- 1 teaspoon ground coriander
- 1/2 teaspoon turmeric powder
- 1/4 teaspoon cayenne pepper (adjust to taste)
- Salt to taste
- Fresh cilantro, chopped (for garnish)
- Cooked rice or naan bread, for serving

Instructions:

1. Heat the vegetable oil in a large skillet or pot over medium heat. Add the chopped onion and cook until softened and translucent, about 5 minutes.
2. Add the minced garlic and grated ginger to the skillet. Cook for another 2 minutes until fragrant.
3. Stir in the chopped tomatoes and cook until they start to soften, about 5 minutes.
4. Add the cubed tempeh to the skillet. Cook until lightly browned on all sides, about 5-7 minutes.
5. Add the assorted vegetables to the skillet. Cook until they are slightly softened, about 5-7 minutes.
6. Add the curry powder, ground cumin, ground coriander, turmeric powder, and cayenne pepper to the skillet. Cook for 1 minute to toast the spices.
7. Pour in the coconut milk. Stir until everything is well combined.
8. Bring the mixture to a simmer, then reduce the heat to low. Cover and let it cook for about 10-15 minutes, stirring occasionally, or until the vegetables are tender and the flavors are melded together.
9. Taste and adjust seasoning with salt if needed.
10. Once the Tempeh Curry is ready, remove from heat and garnish with fresh chopped cilantro.
11. Serve hot with cooked rice or naan bread.

Enjoy the delicious and nutritious Tempeh Curry! Adjust the spiciness according to your preference by adding more or less cayenne pepper.

Cabbage Curry

Ingredients:

- 2 tablespoons vegetable oil
- 1 onion, finely chopped
- 3 cloves garlic, minced
- 1 tablespoon grated ginger
- 1 small head of cabbage, thinly sliced
- 2 tomatoes, chopped
- 1 green chili, chopped (optional, adjust to taste)
- 1 teaspoon mustard seeds
- 1 teaspoon cumin seeds
- 1 teaspoon ground turmeric
- 1 teaspoon ground coriander
- 1/2 teaspoon red chili powder (adjust to taste)
- Salt to taste
- Fresh cilantro, chopped (for garnish)
- Cooked rice or bread, for serving

Instructions:

1. Heat the vegetable oil in a large skillet or pot over medium heat. Add the mustard seeds and cumin seeds. Cook until they start to splutter, about 1 minute.
2. Add the chopped onion and cook until softened and translucent, about 5 minutes.
3. Add the minced garlic, grated ginger, and chopped green chili (if using) to the skillet. Cook for another 2 minutes until fragrant.
4. Stir in the chopped tomatoes and cook until they start to soften, about 5 minutes.
5. Add the thinly sliced cabbage to the skillet. Stir well to combine with the onion and tomato mixture.
6. Add the ground turmeric, ground coriander, and red chili powder to the skillet. Stir well to coat the cabbage with the spices.
7. Cook the cabbage, stirring occasionally, until it is wilted and tender, about 10-15 minutes.
8. Taste and adjust seasoning with salt if needed.
9. Once the Cabbage Curry is ready, remove from heat and garnish with fresh chopped cilantro.
10. Serve hot with cooked rice or bread.

Enjoy the delicious and comforting Cabbage Curry! Feel free to customize it by adding your favorite vegetables or spices.

Bell Pepper Curry

Ingredients:

- 2 tablespoons vegetable oil
- 2 bell peppers (assorted colors), thinly sliced
- 1 onion, finely chopped
- 3 cloves garlic, minced
- 1 tablespoon grated ginger
- 2 tomatoes, chopped
- 1 green chili, chopped (optional, adjust to taste)
- 1 teaspoon mustard seeds
- 1 teaspoon cumin seeds
- 1 teaspoon ground turmeric
- 1 teaspoon ground coriander
- 1/2 teaspoon red chili powder (adjust to taste)
- Salt to taste
- Fresh cilantro, chopped (for garnish)
- Cooked rice or bread, for serving

Instructions:

1. Heat the vegetable oil in a large skillet or pan over medium heat. Add the mustard seeds and cumin seeds. Cook until they start to splutter, about 1 minute.
2. Add the chopped onion and cook until softened and translucent, about 5 minutes.
3. Add the minced garlic, grated ginger, and chopped green chili (if using) to the skillet. Cook for another 2 minutes until fragrant.
4. Stir in the chopped tomatoes and cook until they start to soften, about 5 minutes.
5. Add the thinly sliced bell peppers to the skillet. Stir well to combine with the onion and tomato mixture.
6. Add the ground turmeric, ground coriander, and red chili powder to the skillet. Stir well to coat the bell peppers with the spices.
7. Cook the bell peppers, stirring occasionally, until they are slightly softened but still retain some crunch, about 8-10 minutes.
8. Taste and adjust seasoning with salt if needed.
9. Once the Bell Pepper Curry is ready, remove from heat and garnish with fresh chopped cilantro.
10. Serve hot with cooked rice or bread.

Enjoy the vibrant and flavorful Bell Pepper Curry as a side dish or as a main course! Feel free to adjust the spice level according to your preference.

Chickpea and Cauliflower Curry

Ingredients:

- 2 tablespoons vegetable oil
- 1 onion, finely chopped
- 3 cloves garlic, minced
- 1 tablespoon grated ginger
- 1 head cauliflower, cut into florets
- 1 can (14 oz) chickpeas, drained and rinsed
- 2 tomatoes, chopped
- 1 green chili, chopped (optional, adjust to taste)
- 1 teaspoon mustard seeds
- 1 teaspoon cumin seeds
- 1 teaspoon ground turmeric
- 1 teaspoon ground coriander
- 1/2 teaspoon red chili powder (adjust to taste)
- Salt to taste
- 1 can (14 oz) coconut milk
- Fresh cilantro, chopped (for garnish)
- Cooked rice or naan bread, for serving

Instructions:

1. Heat the vegetable oil in a large skillet or pot over medium heat. Add the mustard seeds and cumin seeds. Cook until they start to splutter, about 1 minute.
2. Add the chopped onion and cook until softened and translucent, about 5 minutes.
3. Add the minced garlic, grated ginger, and chopped green chili (if using) to the skillet. Cook for another 2 minutes until fragrant.
4. Stir in the cauliflower florets and cook for about 5 minutes until they start to soften.
5. Add the drained chickpeas to the skillet. Stir well to combine with the onion and cauliflower mixture.
6. Add the chopped tomatoes to the skillet. Stir well.
7. Add the ground turmeric, ground coriander, and red chili powder to the skillet. Stir well to coat the vegetables with the spices.
8. Pour in the coconut milk. Stir until everything is well combined.
9. Bring the mixture to a simmer, then reduce the heat to low. Cover and let it cook for about 15-20 minutes, stirring occasionally, or until the cauliflower is tender.
10. Taste and adjust seasoning with salt if needed.
11. Once the Chickpea and Cauliflower Curry is ready, remove from heat and garnish with fresh chopped cilantro.
12. Serve hot with cooked rice or naan bread.

Enjoy the delicious and nutritious Chickpea and Cauliflower Curry! Adjust the spice level according to your preference by adding more or less red chili powder.

Coconut Chickpea Curry

Ingredients:

- 2 tablespoons vegetable oil
- 1 onion, finely chopped
- 3 cloves garlic, minced
- 1 tablespoon grated ginger
- 2 tomatoes, chopped
- 2 cans (14 oz each) chickpeas, drained and rinsed
- 1 can (14 oz) coconut milk
- 1 tablespoon curry powder
- 1 teaspoon ground cumin
- 1 teaspoon ground coriander
- 1/2 teaspoon turmeric powder
- 1/4 teaspoon cayenne pepper (adjust to taste)
- Salt to taste
- Fresh cilantro, chopped (for garnish)
- Cooked rice or naan bread, for serving

Instructions:

1. Heat the vegetable oil in a large skillet or pot over medium heat. Add the chopped onion and cook until softened and translucent, about 5 minutes.
2. Add the minced garlic and grated ginger to the skillet. Cook for another 2 minutes until fragrant.
3. Stir in the chopped tomatoes and cook until they start to soften, about 5 minutes.
4. Add the drained chickpeas to the skillet. Stir well to combine with the onion and tomato mixture.
5. Add the curry powder, ground cumin, ground coriander, turmeric powder, and cayenne pepper to the skillet. Cook for 1 minute to toast the spices.
6. Pour in the coconut milk. Stir until everything is well combined.
7. Bring the mixture to a simmer, then reduce the heat to low. Cover and let it cook for about 15-20 minutes, stirring occasionally, to allow the flavors to meld together and the sauce to thicken.
8. Taste and adjust seasoning with salt if needed.
9. Once the Coconut Chickpea Curry is ready, remove from heat and garnish with fresh chopped cilantro.
10. Serve hot with cooked rice or naan bread.

Enjoy the creamy and flavorful Coconut Chickpea Curry! Adjust the spiciness according to your preference by adding more or less cayenne pepper.

Peanut Curry

Ingredients:

- 2 tablespoons vegetable oil
- 1 onion, finely chopped
- 3 cloves garlic, minced
- 1 tablespoon grated ginger
- 2 tomatoes, chopped
- 1/2 cup peanut butter (smooth or chunky)
- 2 cups vegetable broth or water
- 1 sweet potato, peeled and diced
- 1 can (14 oz) chickpeas, drained and rinsed
- 1 cup chopped spinach or kale
- 1 teaspoon curry powder
- 1 teaspoon ground cumin
- 1/2 teaspoon ground coriander
- 1/2 teaspoon paprika
- 1/4 teaspoon cayenne pepper (adjust to taste)
- Salt to taste
- Fresh cilantro, chopped (for garnish)
- Cooked rice or crusty bread, for serving

Instructions:

1. Heat the vegetable oil in a large pot or Dutch oven over medium heat. Add the chopped onion and cook until softened and translucent, about 5 minutes.
2. Add the minced garlic and grated ginger to the pot. Cook for another 2 minutes until fragrant.
3. Stir in the chopped tomatoes and cook until they start to soften, about 5 minutes.
4. Add the peanut butter to the pot and stir until it's melted and well combined with the onion and tomato mixture.
5. Gradually pour in the vegetable broth or water, stirring continuously to create a smooth sauce.
6. Add the diced sweet potato and drained chickpeas to the pot. Stir well to combine.
7. Add the curry powder, ground cumin, ground coriander, paprika, and cayenne pepper to the pot. Stir well to evenly distribute the spices.
8. Bring the mixture to a simmer, then reduce the heat to low. Cover and let it cook for about 20-25 minutes, stirring occasionally, or until the sweet potatoes are tender.
9. Stir in the chopped spinach or kale and cook for an additional 5 minutes until wilted.
10. Taste and adjust seasoning with salt if needed.
11. Once the Peanut Curry is ready, remove from heat and garnish with fresh chopped cilantro.
12. Serve hot with cooked rice or crusty bread.

Enjoy the rich and comforting Peanut Curry! Adjust the spiciness according to your preference by adding more or less cayenne pepper.

Beetroot Curry

Ingredients:

- 2 tablespoons vegetable oil
- 1 onion, finely chopped
- 3 cloves garlic, minced
- 1 tablespoon grated ginger
- 2 medium-sized beetroots, peeled and diced
- 2 tomatoes, chopped
- 1 green chili, chopped (optional, adjust to taste)
- 1 teaspoon mustard seeds
- 1 teaspoon cumin seeds
- 1 teaspoon ground turmeric
- 1 teaspoon ground coriander
- 1/2 teaspoon red chili powder (adjust to taste)
- Salt to taste
- 1 cup coconut milk or yogurt (optional for creaminess)
- Fresh cilantro, chopped (for garnish)
- Cooked rice or bread, for serving

Instructions:

1. Heat the vegetable oil in a large skillet or pot over medium heat. Add the mustard seeds and cumin seeds. Cook until they start to splutter, about 1 minute.
2. Add the chopped onion and cook until softened and translucent, about 5 minutes.
3. Add the minced garlic, grated ginger, and chopped green chili (if using) to the skillet. Cook for another 2 minutes until fragrant.
4. Stir in the diced beetroots and cook for about 5 minutes until they start to soften.
5. Add the chopped tomatoes to the skillet. Stir well.
6. Add the ground turmeric, ground coriander, and red chili powder to the skillet. Stir well to coat the beetroots with the spices.
7. Pour in about 1/2 cup of water. Cover and let it cook for about 15-20 minutes, or until the beetroots are tender, stirring occasionally and adding more water if needed to prevent sticking.
8. Once the beetroots are cooked, stir in the coconut milk or yogurt if using. Cook for an additional 2-3 minutes to heat through.
9. Taste and adjust seasoning with salt if needed.

10. Once the Beetroot Curry is ready, remove from heat and garnish with fresh chopped cilantro.
11. Serve hot with cooked rice or bread.

Enjoy the unique and flavorful Beetroot Curry! Adjust the spice level according to your preference by adding more or less red chili powder.

Quinoa Curry

Ingredients:

- 1 cup quinoa, rinsed
- 2 cups vegetable broth or water
- 2 tablespoons vegetable oil
- 1 onion, finely chopped
- 3 cloves garlic, minced
- 1 tablespoon grated ginger
- 2 tomatoes, chopped
- Assorted vegetables (such as bell peppers, carrots, peas, etc.), chopped or sliced
- 1 can (14 oz) chickpeas, drained and rinsed
- 1 can (14 oz) coconut milk
- 1 tablespoon curry powder
- 1 teaspoon ground cumin
- 1 teaspoon ground coriander
- 1/2 teaspoon turmeric powder
- 1/4 teaspoon cayenne pepper (adjust to taste)
- Salt to taste
- Fresh cilantro, chopped (for garnish)
- Cooked quinoa or rice, for serving

Instructions:

1. In a medium saucepan, combine the rinsed quinoa and vegetable broth or water. Bring to a boil, then reduce the heat to low, cover, and simmer for about 15-20 minutes, or until the quinoa is cooked and the liquid is absorbed. Remove from heat and set aside.
2. In a large skillet or pot, heat the vegetable oil over medium heat. Add the chopped onion and cook until softened and translucent, about 5 minutes.
3. Add the minced garlic and grated ginger to the skillet. Cook for another 2 minutes until fragrant.
4. Stir in the chopped tomatoes and cook until they start to soften, about 5 minutes.
5. Add the assorted vegetables to the skillet. Cook until they are slightly softened, about 5-7 minutes.
6. Add the drained chickpeas to the skillet. Stir well to combine with the onion and vegetable mixture.

7. Add the curry powder, ground cumin, ground coriander, turmeric powder, and cayenne pepper to the skillet. Cook for 1 minute to toast the spices.
8. Pour in the coconut milk. Stir until everything is well combined.
9. Bring the mixture to a simmer, then reduce the heat to low. Cover and let it cook for about 10-15 minutes, stirring occasionally, or until the vegetables are tender and the flavors are melded together.
10. Taste and adjust seasoning with salt if needed.
11. Once the curry is ready, serve it over cooked quinoa or rice.
12. Garnish with fresh chopped cilantro before serving.

Enjoy the flavorful and nutritious Quinoa Curry as a hearty main dish! Feel free to customize it by adding your favorite vegetables or adjusting the spice level to your preference.

Lentil and Pumpkin Curry

Ingredients:

- 1 cup dried lentils (brown or green), rinsed
- 2 cups vegetable broth or water
- 2 tablespoons vegetable oil
- 1 onion, finely chopped
- 3 cloves garlic, minced
- 1 tablespoon grated ginger
- 2 cups pumpkin or butternut squash, peeled and diced
- 2 tomatoes, chopped
- 1 can (14 oz) coconut milk
- 1 tablespoon curry powder
- 1 teaspoon ground cumin
- 1 teaspoon ground coriander
- 1/2 teaspoon turmeric powder
- 1/4 teaspoon cayenne pepper (adjust to taste)
- Salt to taste
- Fresh cilantro, chopped (for garnish)
- Cooked rice or naan bread, for serving

Instructions:

1. In a medium saucepan, combine the rinsed lentils and vegetable broth or water. Bring to a boil, then reduce the heat to low, cover, and simmer for about 20-25 minutes, or until the lentils are tender. Remove from heat and set aside.
2. In a large skillet or pot, heat the vegetable oil over medium heat. Add the chopped onion and cook until softened and translucent, about 5 minutes.
3. Add the minced garlic and grated ginger to the skillet. Cook for another 2 minutes until fragrant.
4. Stir in the diced pumpkin or butternut squash and cook for about 5 minutes until they start to soften.
5. Add the chopped tomatoes to the skillet. Stir well.
6. Add the cooked lentils to the skillet, along with any remaining cooking liquid.
7. Add the curry powder, ground cumin, ground coriander, turmeric powder, and cayenne pepper to the skillet. Stir well to coat the vegetables and lentils with the spices.
8. Pour in the coconut milk. Stir until everything is well combined.
9. Bring the mixture to a simmer, then reduce the heat to low. Cover and let it cook for about 10-15 minutes, stirring occasionally, to allow the flavors to meld together and the pumpkin to become tender.
10. Taste and adjust seasoning with salt if needed.

11. Once the Lentil and Pumpkin Curry is ready, remove from heat and garnish with fresh chopped cilantro.
12. Serve hot with cooked rice or naan bread.

Enjoy the hearty and flavorful Lentil and Pumpkin Curry! Adjust the spiciness according to your preference by adding more or less cayenne pepper.

Turmeric Tofu Curry

Ingredients:

- 1 block (14 oz) extra-firm tofu, pressed and cubed
- 2 tablespoons vegetable oil
- 1 onion, finely chopped
- 3 cloves garlic, minced
- 1 tablespoon grated ginger
- 2 tomatoes, chopped
- 1 can (14 oz) coconut milk
- 1 tablespoon curry powder
- 1 teaspoon ground cumin
- 1 teaspoon ground coriander
- 1 teaspoon ground turmeric
- 1/4 teaspoon cayenne pepper (adjust to taste)
- Salt to taste
- Fresh cilantro, chopped (for garnish)
- Cooked rice or naan bread, for serving

Instructions:

1. Heat 1 tablespoon of vegetable oil in a large skillet or non-stick pan over medium-high heat. Add the cubed tofu and cook until golden brown on all sides, about 8-10 minutes. Remove tofu from the skillet and set aside.
2. In the same skillet, add the remaining tablespoon of vegetable oil. Add the chopped onion and cook until softened and translucent, about 5 minutes.
3. Add the minced garlic and grated ginger to the skillet. Cook for another 2 minutes until fragrant.
4. Stir in the chopped tomatoes and cook until they start to soften, about 5 minutes.
5. Add the curry powder, ground cumin, ground coriander, ground turmeric, and cayenne pepper to the skillet. Cook for 1 minute to toast the spices.
6. Pour in the coconut milk. Stir until everything is well combined.
7. Bring the mixture to a simmer, then reduce the heat to low. Cover and let it cook for about 10 minutes, stirring occasionally.
8. Add the cooked tofu to the skillet and stir gently to coat it with the curry sauce. Let it simmer for an additional 5 minutes to heat through.
9. Taste and adjust seasoning with salt if needed.

10. Once the Turmeric Tofu Curry is ready, remove from heat and garnish with fresh chopped cilantro.
11. Serve hot with cooked rice or naan bread.

Enjoy the creamy and aromatic Turmeric Tofu Curry! Adjust the spiciness according to your preference by adding more or less cayenne pepper.

Vegan Rogan Josh

Ingredients:

- 2 tablespoons vegetable oil
- 1 onion, finely chopped
- 3 cloves garlic, minced
- 1 tablespoon grated ginger
- 2 tomatoes, chopped
- 1 red bell pepper, diced
- 1 cup cauliflower florets
- 1 cup diced potatoes
- 1 cup diced carrots
- 1 can (14 oz) chickpeas, drained and rinsed
- 1 can (14 oz) coconut milk
- 1 tablespoon tomato paste
- 1 tablespoon curry powder
- 1 teaspoon ground cumin
- 1 teaspoon ground coriander
- 1 teaspoon paprika
- 1/2 teaspoon ground cinnamon
- 1/2 teaspoon ground cardamom
- 1/4 teaspoon cayenne pepper (adjust to taste)
- Salt to taste
- Fresh cilantro, chopped (for garnish)
- Cooked rice or naan bread, for serving

Instructions:

1. Heat the vegetable oil in a large skillet or pot over medium heat. Add the chopped onion and cook until softened and translucent, about 5 minutes.
2. Add the minced garlic and grated ginger to the skillet. Cook for another 2 minutes until fragrant.
3. Stir in the chopped tomatoes and cook until they start to soften, about 5 minutes.
4. Add the diced red bell pepper, cauliflower florets, diced potatoes, and diced carrots to the skillet. Stir well to combine.
5. Add the drained chickpeas to the skillet. Stir again.
6. In a small bowl, mix together the tomato paste, curry powder, ground cumin, ground coriander, paprika, ground cinnamon, ground cardamom, and cayenne pepper.
7. Add the spice mixture to the skillet. Stir until everything is well coated.
8. Pour in the coconut milk. Stir until everything is well combined.
9. Bring the mixture to a simmer, then reduce the heat to low. Cover and let it cook for about 20-25 minutes, or until the vegetables are tender and the flavors have melded together.

10. Taste and adjust seasoning with salt if needed.
11. Once the Vegan Rogan Josh is ready, remove from heat and garnish with fresh chopped cilantro.
12. Serve hot with cooked rice or naan bread.

Enjoy the rich and aromatic Vegan Rogan Josh! Adjust the spiciness according to your preference by adding more or less cayenne pepper.

Green Bean Curry

Ingredients:

- 2 tablespoons vegetable oil
- 1 onion, finely chopped
- 3 cloves garlic, minced
- 1 tablespoon grated ginger
- 2 tomatoes, chopped
- 1 pound green beans, trimmed and cut into bite-sized pieces
- 1 can (14 oz) coconut milk
- 1 tablespoon curry powder
- 1 teaspoon ground cumin
- 1 teaspoon ground coriander
- 1/2 teaspoon turmeric powder
- 1/4 teaspoon cayenne pepper (adjust to taste)
- Salt to taste
- Fresh cilantro, chopped (for garnish)
- Cooked rice or naan bread, for serving

Instructions:

1. Heat the vegetable oil in a large skillet or pot over medium heat. Add the chopped onion and cook until softened and translucent, about 5 minutes.
2. Add the minced garlic and grated ginger to the skillet. Cook for another 2 minutes until fragrant.
3. Stir in the chopped tomatoes and cook until they start to soften, about 5 minutes.
4. Add the green beans to the skillet. Stir well to combine with the onion and tomato mixture.
5. Add the curry powder, ground cumin, ground coriander, turmeric powder, and cayenne pepper to the skillet. Stir well to coat the green beans with the spices.
6. Pour in the coconut milk. Stir until everything is well combined.
7. Bring the mixture to a simmer, then reduce the heat to low. Cover and let it cook for about 10-15 minutes, or until the green beans are tender but still crisp.
8. Taste and adjust seasoning with salt if needed.
9. Once the Green Bean Curry is ready, remove from heat and garnish with fresh chopped cilantro.
10. Serve hot with cooked rice or naan bread.

Enjoy the delicious and vibrant Green Bean Curry! Adjust the spiciness according to your preference by adding more or less cayenne pepper.

Tamarind Curry

Ingredients:

- 2 tablespoons vegetable oil
- 1 onion, finely chopped
- 3 cloves garlic, minced
- 1 tablespoon grated ginger
- 2 tomatoes, chopped
- 1 cup mixed vegetables (such as bell peppers, carrots, potatoes, peas, etc.), chopped or sliced
- 1 can (14 oz) coconut milk
- 2 tablespoons tamarind paste
- 1 tablespoon brown sugar or maple syrup
- 1 tablespoon curry powder
- 1 teaspoon ground cumin
- 1 teaspoon ground coriander
- 1/2 teaspoon turmeric powder
- 1/4 teaspoon cayenne pepper (adjust to taste)
- Salt to taste
- Fresh cilantro, chopped (for garnish)
- Cooked rice or naan bread, for serving

Instructions:

1. Heat the vegetable oil in a large skillet or pot over medium heat. Add the chopped onion and cook until softened and translucent, about 5 minutes.
2. Add the minced garlic and grated ginger to the skillet. Cook for another 2 minutes until fragrant.
3. Stir in the chopped tomatoes and cook until they start to soften, about 5 minutes.
4. Add the mixed vegetables to the skillet. Stir well to combine with the onion and tomato mixture.
5. In a small bowl, mix together the tamarind paste, brown sugar or maple syrup, curry powder, ground cumin, ground coriander, turmeric powder, and cayenne pepper.
6. Add the spice mixture to the skillet. Stir well to coat the vegetables.
7. Pour in the coconut milk. Stir until everything is well combined.
8. Bring the mixture to a simmer, then reduce the heat to low. Cover and let it cook for about 15-20 minutes, or until the vegetables are tender and the flavors have melded together.
9. Taste and adjust seasoning with salt if needed.
10. Once the Tamarind Curry is ready, remove from heat and garnish with fresh chopped cilantro.
11. Serve hot with cooked rice or naan bread.

Enjoy the tangy and flavorful Tamarind Curry! Adjust the spiciness according to your preference by adding more or less cayenne pepper.

Vegan Paneer Curry (with tofu or paneer substitute)

Ingredients:

- 1 block (14 oz) extra-firm tofu, pressed and cubed (or vegan paneer substitute of your choice)
- 2 tablespoons vegetable oil
- 1 onion, finely chopped
- 3 cloves garlic, minced
- 1 tablespoon grated ginger
- 2 tomatoes, chopped
- 1 cup coconut milk
- 1 tablespoon tomato paste
- 1 tablespoon curry powder
- 1 teaspoon ground cumin
- 1 teaspoon ground coriander
- 1 teaspoon garam masala
- 1/2 teaspoon turmeric powder
- 1/4 teaspoon cayenne pepper (adjust to taste)
- Salt to taste
- Fresh cilantro, chopped (for garnish)
- Cooked rice or naan bread, for serving

Instructions:

1. Heat the vegetable oil in a large skillet or pan over medium heat. Add the cubed tofu and cook until golden brown on all sides, about 8-10 minutes. Remove tofu from the skillet and set aside.
2. In the same skillet, add a bit more oil if needed. Add the chopped onion and cook until softened and translucent, about 5 minutes.
3. Add the minced garlic and grated ginger to the skillet. Cook for another 2 minutes until fragrant.
4. Stir in the chopped tomatoes and cook until they start to soften, about 5 minutes.
5. Add the tomato paste, curry powder, ground cumin, ground coriander, garam masala, turmeric powder, and cayenne pepper to the skillet. Cook for 1 minute to toast the spices.
6. Pour in the coconut milk. Stir until everything is well combined.
7. Bring the mixture to a simmer, then reduce the heat to low. Cover and let it cook for about 10 minutes, stirring occasionally.
8. Taste and adjust seasoning with salt if needed.
9. Add the cooked tofu to the skillet and stir gently to coat it with the curry sauce. Let it simmer for an additional 5 minutes to heat through.
10. Once the Vegan Paneer Curry is ready, remove from heat and garnish with fresh chopped cilantro.

11. Serve hot with cooked rice or naan bread.

Enjoy the creamy and flavorful Vegan Paneer Curry! Adjust the spiciness according to your preference by adding more or less cayenne pepper.

Brussels Sprouts Curry

Ingredients:

- 2 tablespoons vegetable oil
- 1 onion, finely chopped
- 3 cloves garlic, minced
- 1 tablespoon grated ginger
- 2 tomatoes, chopped
- 1 pound Brussels sprouts, trimmed and halved
- 1 can (14 oz) coconut milk
- 1 tablespoon curry powder
- 1 teaspoon ground cumin
- 1 teaspoon ground coriander
- 1/2 teaspoon turmeric powder
- 1/4 teaspoon cayenne pepper (adjust to taste)
- Salt to taste
- Fresh cilantro, chopped (for garnish)
- Cooked rice or naan bread, for serving

Instructions:

1. Heat the vegetable oil in a large skillet or pot over medium heat. Add the chopped onion and cook until softened and translucent, about 5 minutes.
2. Add the minced garlic and grated ginger to the skillet. Cook for another 2 minutes until fragrant.
3. Stir in the chopped tomatoes and cook until they start to soften, about 5 minutes.
4. Add the Brussels sprouts to the skillet. Stir well to combine with the onion and tomato mixture.
5. Add the curry powder, ground cumin, ground coriander, turmeric powder, and cayenne pepper to the skillet. Stir well to coat the Brussels sprouts with the spices.
6. Pour in the coconut milk. Stir until everything is well combined.
7. Bring the mixture to a simmer, then reduce the heat to low. Cover and let it cook for about 15-20 minutes, or until the Brussels sprouts are tender.
8. Taste and adjust seasoning with salt if needed.
9. Once the Brussels Sprouts Curry is ready, remove from heat and garnish with fresh chopped cilantro.
10. Serve hot with cooked rice or naan bread.

Enjoy the delicious and flavorful Brussels Sprouts Curry! Adjust the spiciness according to your preference by adding more or less cayenne pepper.

Avocado Curry

Ingredients:

- 2 ripe avocados, peeled, pitted, and diced
- 2 tablespoons vegetable oil
- 1 onion, finely chopped
- 3 cloves garlic, minced
- 1 tablespoon grated ginger
- 2 tomatoes, chopped
- 1 can (14 oz) coconut milk
- 1 tablespoon curry powder
- 1 teaspoon ground cumin
- 1 teaspoon ground coriander
- 1/2 teaspoon turmeric powder
- 1/4 teaspoon cayenne pepper (adjust to taste)
- Salt to taste
- Fresh cilantro, chopped (for garnish)
- Cooked rice or naan bread, for serving

Instructions:

1. Heat the vegetable oil in a large skillet or pot over medium heat. Add the chopped onion and cook until softened and translucent, about 5 minutes.
2. Add the minced garlic and grated ginger to the skillet. Cook for another 2 minutes until fragrant.
3. Stir in the chopped tomatoes and cook until they start to soften, about 5 minutes.
4. Add the diced avocados to the skillet. Stir well to combine with the onion and tomato mixture.
5. Add the curry powder, ground cumin, ground coriander, turmeric powder, and cayenne pepper to the skillet. Stir well to coat the avocados with the spices.
6. Pour in the coconut milk. Stir until everything is well combined.
7. Bring the mixture to a simmer, then reduce the heat to low. Cover and let it cook for about 10-15 minutes, stirring occasionally.
8. Taste and adjust seasoning with salt if needed.
9. Once the Avocado Curry is ready, remove from heat and garnish with fresh chopped cilantro.
10. Serve hot with cooked rice or naan bread.

Enjoy the creamy and flavorful Avocado Curry! Adjust the spiciness according to your preference by adding more or less cayenne pepper.

Mango Curry

Ingredients:

- 2 ripe mangoes, peeled, pitted, and diced
- 2 tablespoons vegetable oil
- 1 onion, finely chopped
- 3 cloves garlic, minced
- 1 tablespoon grated ginger
- 2 tomatoes, chopped
- 1 can (14 oz) coconut milk
- 1 tablespoon curry powder
- 1 teaspoon ground cumin
- 1 teaspoon ground coriander
- 1/2 teaspoon turmeric powder
- 1/4 teaspoon cayenne pepper (adjust to taste)
- Salt to taste
- Fresh cilantro, chopped (for garnish)
- Cooked rice or naan bread, for serving

Instructions:

1. Heat the vegetable oil in a large skillet or pot over medium heat. Add the chopped onion and cook until softened and translucent, about 5 minutes.
2. Add the minced garlic and grated ginger to the skillet. Cook for another 2 minutes until fragrant.
3. Stir in the chopped tomatoes and cook until they start to soften, about 5 minutes.
4. Add the diced mangoes to the skillet. Stir well to combine with the onion and tomato mixture.
5. Add the curry powder, ground cumin, ground coriander, turmeric powder, and cayenne pepper to the skillet. Stir well to coat the mangoes with the spices.
6. Pour in the coconut milk. Stir until everything is well combined.
7. Bring the mixture to a simmer, then reduce the heat to low. Cover and let it cook for about 10-15 minutes, stirring occasionally.
8. Taste and adjust seasoning with salt if needed.
9. Once the Mango Curry is ready, remove from heat and garnish with fresh chopped cilantro.
10. Serve hot with cooked rice or naan bread.

Enjoy the sweet and tangy Mango Curry! Adjust the spiciness according to your preference by adding more or less cayenne pepper.

Vegan Bhuna

Ingredients:

- 2 tablespoons vegetable oil
- 1 onion, finely chopped
- 3 cloves garlic, minced
- 1 tablespoon grated ginger
- 2 tomatoes, chopped
- 1 bell pepper, diced
- 1 cup mixed vegetables (such as carrots, peas, cauliflower, etc.), chopped or sliced
- 1 can (14 oz) chickpeas, drained and rinsed
- 1 tablespoon tomato paste
- 1 tablespoon curry powder
- 1 teaspoon ground cumin
- 1 teaspoon ground coriander
- 1/2 teaspoon turmeric powder
- 1/4 teaspoon cayenne pepper (adjust to taste)
- Salt to taste
- Fresh cilantro, chopped (for garnish)
- Cooked rice or naan bread, for serving

Instructions:

1. Heat the vegetable oil in a large skillet or pot over medium heat. Add the chopped onion and cook until softened and translucent, about 5 minutes.
2. Add the minced garlic and grated ginger to the skillet. Cook for another 2 minutes until fragrant.
3. Stir in the chopped tomatoes and bell pepper. Cook until they start to soften, about 5 minutes.
4. Add the mixed vegetables to the skillet. Stir well to combine with the onion and tomato mixture.
5. Add the chickpeas to the skillet. Stir again.
6. In a small bowl, mix together the tomato paste, curry powder, ground cumin, ground coriander, turmeric powder, and cayenne pepper.
7. Add the spice mixture to the skillet. Stir well to coat the vegetables and chickpeas.
8. Pour in a splash of water to deglaze the pan and prevent sticking.
9. Cook for 10-15 minutes over medium heat, stirring occasionally, until the vegetables are tender and the sauce has thickened.
10. Taste and adjust seasoning with salt if needed.
11. Once the Vegan Bhuna is ready, remove from heat and garnish with fresh chopped cilantro.
12. Serve hot with cooked rice or naan bread.

Enjoy the spicy and flavorful Vegan Bhuna! Adjust the spiciness according to your preference by adding more or less cayenne pepper.

Ratatouille Curry

Ingredients:

- 1 large eggplant, diced
- 2 zucchinis, diced
- 1 bell pepper, diced
- 1 onion, diced
- 3 tomatoes, diced
- 3 cloves garlic, minced
- 2 tablespoons curry powder
- 1 teaspoon ground cumin
- 1 teaspoon ground coriander
- 1/2 teaspoon turmeric powder
- Salt and pepper to taste
- Olive oil
- Fresh basil leaves for garnish (optional)

Instructions:

1. Heat some olive oil in a large skillet or pot over medium heat.
2. Add the diced onion and minced garlic to the skillet. Sauté until the onion is translucent and fragrant, about 3-4 minutes.
3. Add the diced eggplant, zucchini, and bell pepper to the skillet. Cook for about 5 minutes, stirring occasionally, until the vegetables start to soften.
4. Stir in the diced tomatoes, curry powder, ground cumin, ground coriander, turmeric powder, salt, and pepper. Mix well to combine all the flavors.
5. Cover the skillet and let the curry simmer over medium-low heat for about 15-20 minutes, or until all the vegetables are tender and the flavors have melded together, stirring occasionally.
6. Once the curry is cooked to your desired consistency and the vegetables are tender, remove it from heat.
7. Serve the Ratatouille Curry hot, garnished with fresh basil leaves if desired. It can be enjoyed on its own, with rice, quinoa, or crusty bread.

This Ratatouille Curry is a flavorful and satisfying dish that combines the best of both French and Indian cuisines. Feel free to adjust the spices and seasonings according to your taste preferences. Enjoy!

Lemon and Lentil Curry

Ingredients:

- 1 cup dried red lentils
- 1 onion, finely chopped
- 3 cloves garlic, minced
- 1-inch piece of ginger, grated
- 2 tomatoes, chopped
- 1 can (400ml) coconut milk
- 2 cups vegetable broth or water
- 1 lemon (juice and zest)
- 2 teaspoons curry powder
- 1 teaspoon ground turmeric
- 1 teaspoon ground cumin
- 1 teaspoon ground coriander
- 1/2 teaspoon chili powder (adjust to taste)
- Salt and pepper to taste
- Fresh cilantro leaves for garnish
- Cooked rice or naan bread for serving

Instructions:

1. Rinse the lentils under cold water until the water runs clear. Drain and set aside.
2. Heat some oil in a large pot over medium heat. Add the chopped onion and cook until softened, about 5 minutes.
3. Add the minced garlic and grated ginger to the pot. Cook for another 2 minutes, stirring frequently.
4. Stir in the curry powder, ground turmeric, ground cumin, ground coriander, and chili powder. Cook for 1 minute until fragrant.
5. Add the chopped tomatoes to the pot and cook for 5 minutes, stirring occasionally, until they start to break down.
6. Pour in the coconut milk and vegetable broth (or water). Stir well to combine.
7. Add the rinsed lentils to the pot. Bring the mixture to a simmer, then reduce the heat to low. Cover and let it cook for about 20-25 minutes, or until the lentils are tender and the curry has thickened, stirring occasionally.
8. Once the lentils are cooked, stir in the lemon juice and zest. Season with salt and pepper to taste.
9. Serve the Lemon and Lentil Curry hot, garnished with fresh cilantro leaves. Enjoy with cooked rice or naan bread.

This Lemon and Lentil Curry is tangy, aromatic, and full of comforting flavors. It's perfect for a cozy meal any day of the week! Feel free to adjust the seasoning and spices according to your taste preferences. Enjoy!

Vegan Jalfrezi

Ingredients:

- 2 tablespoons vegetable oil
- 1 onion, thinly sliced
- 2 bell peppers (any color), sliced
- 1 cup cauliflower florets
- 1 cup diced carrots
- 1 cup diced potatoes
- 2 tomatoes, diced
- 3 cloves garlic, minced
- 1-inch piece of ginger, grated
- 2 green chilies, sliced (adjust to taste)
- 2 teaspoons ground cumin
- 2 teaspoons ground coriander
- 1 teaspoon turmeric powder
- 1 teaspoon paprika
- 1 teaspoon garam masala
- Salt to taste
- Fresh cilantro leaves for garnish

Instructions:

1. Heat the vegetable oil in a large pan or wok over medium heat.
2. Add the thinly sliced onion to the pan and cook until softened and translucent, about 5 minutes.
3. Add the minced garlic, grated ginger, and sliced green chilies to the pan. Stir-fry for another 2 minutes until fragrant.
4. Add the sliced bell peppers, cauliflower florets, diced carrots, and diced potatoes to the pan. Stir well to combine with the onions and spices.
5. Cook the vegetables for about 8-10 minutes, stirring occasionally, until they start to soften but are still slightly crisp.
6. Stir in the diced tomatoes, ground cumin, ground coriander, turmeric powder, paprika, and garam masala. Mix well to coat the vegetables with the spices.
7. Cook the mixture for another 5-7 minutes, or until the tomatoes have softened and the flavors have melded together. If the mixture starts to stick to the pan, you can add a splash of water.
8. Season the Vegan Jalfrezi with salt to taste, and garnish with fresh cilantro leaves.

9. Serve the Vegan Jalfrezi hot with rice or naan bread.

This Vegan Jalfrezi is bursting with flavor and packed with nutritious vegetables. It's a satisfying and wholesome dish that's sure to please everyone at the table, whether they're vegan or not. Enjoy!

www.ingramcontent.com/pod-product-compliance
Lightning Source LLC
LaVergne TN
LVHW062048070526
838201LV00080B/2259